Official
Cambridge
Exam
Preparation

Official Quick Guide to Linguaskill

Karen Ludlow

T0363861

Cambridge University Press
www.cambridge.org/elt

Cambridge Assessment English
www.cambridgeenglish.org

Information on this title: www.cambridge.org/9781108885256

First published 2020

20 19 18 17 16 15 14 13 12 11 10 9 8 7 6 5 4 3 2 1

Printed in Poland by Opolgraf

A catalogue record for this publication is available from the British Library

ISBN 978-1-108-88525-6

The publishers have no responsibility for the persistence or accuracy
of URLs for external or third-party internet websites referred to in this publication,
and does not guarantee that any content on such websites is, or will remain,
accurate or appropriate. Information regarding prices, travel timetables, and other
factual information given in this work is correct at the time of first printing but
the publishers do not guarantee the accuracy of such information thereafter.

Useful links for the Linguaskill test

You can access these links for more information and do practice tests online:

https://www.cambridgeenglish.org/exams-and-tests/linguaskill/

https://www.cambridgeenglish.org/exams-and-tests/linguaskill/information-about-the-test/practice-materials/

The practice tests under the section Linguaskill General and Business practice tests are divided into Elementary, Intermediate and Advanced. **They are not adaptive** and don't give you a level. They have an answer key with a score and they offer useful information about why an answer is correct or not. They give you practice of the question types you have seen in this information booklet.

The free online sample tests **do not give a score or save answers**. The Listening and Reading test is **shorter** than a real online Linguaskill test.

https://writeandimprove.com

https://speakandimprove.com

Write and Improve and *Speak and Improve* are free online tools to help you practise and develop these skills for tests like Linguaskill or any other exams you are taking.

Contents

Overview of the Linguaskill test 4

Listening and Reading module 8

Writing module 9

Speaking module 9

Linguaskill in the future 10

Preparing for and taking Linguaskill 11

Example questions, tasks and tips 14

 Listening and Reading 14

 Writing 22

 Speaking 24

Example tasks and tips answer key 34

What is Cambridge Assessment English Linguaskill?

Cambridge Assessment English Linguaskill is an online test which checks your level of English as an individual or as a group of people. It has different **modules** and it tests reading, listening, writing and speaking. As the test is **modular** it means you or an organisation (your workplace or study centre) can choose which of the four areas you want to test to find out your level of English. For example, you can test all four main skills or only one or two of them.

There are two test options: **General** and **Business**. You can choose the type of test you take based on your English needs or objectives. (See **Test options**, page 5.)

Where and when can I take Linguaskill?

Linguaskill is flexible so you can take it at any time and at any place with an organisation that administers the test. To take the test you need a computer, an internet connection, a microphone and a set of headphones.

What is the test format and approximate time for each module?

Listening and Reading are tested together in one module. This part of the test is **adaptive**. The computer will **adapt** the questions to what you can do in order to evaluate your level of English. This means that the questions you answer will become easier or more difficult based on the answer you gave to a question you answered before.

Test format	
📄🎧	Reading and Listening (combined) **60–85 minutes** approximately
✏️	Writing **45 minutes**
🎧	Speaking **15 minutes** approximately

Test options

General English

This tests English in daily life and topics may include studying, future plans, travel, technology and work. You don't need to know any specific language about the world of work or business. If you are a general English student or planning to study at university, this test is the best option for you.

Business English

This tests English in a business context and topics may include buying and selling different products or services, situations in the office, business travel and human resources, etc. If you are going to apply for a specific job or you are already working and your company/organisation wants to test your level of English, this test is the best option for you.

How is the test graded and how do I get my results?

Linguaskill gives you fast and accurate results. You can get your results for the Listening and Reading module as soon as you finish the test and results for all other modules within 48 hours – although in most cases it will be sooner than this.

Instead of a printed certificate you will get a **Test Report Form** which is generated automatically. You may also see your results directly online if the place or institution where you take the test authorises this.

Linguaskill uses the Common European Framework of Reference for Languages (CEFR) to give you a grade from A1 or below to C1 or above. The CEFR is an international standard that helps you to understand your ability, or what you **can do**, in a language. You can compare your Linguaskill results to international standards. Each CEFR level is linked to test scores in the Linguaskill test.

For more information about the CEFR go to https://www.cambridgeenglish.org/exams-and-tests/cefr/

Score	CEFR
180+	C1 or above
160–179	B2
140–159	B1
120–139	A2
100–119	A1
82–99	Below A1

The Test Report Form shows:

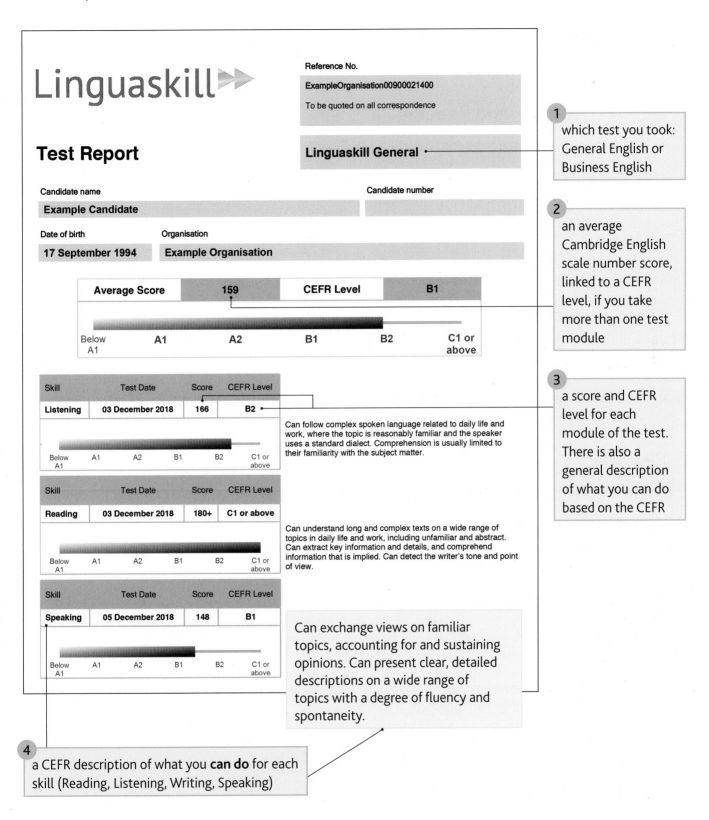

Linguaskill ▶▶

Reference No.
ExampleOrganisation00900021400
To be quoted on all correspondence

Linguaskill General •

1 which test you took: General English or Business English

Test Report

Candidate name
Example Candidate

Candidate number

Date of birth
17 September 1994

Organisation
Example Organisation

2 an average Cambridge English scale number score, linked to a CEFR level, if you take more than one test module

| Average Score | 159 | CEFR Level | B1 |

Below A1 — A1 — A2 — B1 — B2 — C1 or above

| Skill | Test Date | Score | CEFR Level |
| Listening | 03 December 2018 | 166 | B2 • |

Below A1 — A1 — A2 — B1 — B2 — C1 or above

Can follow complex spoken language related to daily life and work, where the topic is reasonably familiar and the speaker uses a standard dialect. Comprehension is usually limited to their familiarity with the subject matter.

3 a score and CEFR level for each module of the test. There is also a general description of what you can do based on the CEFR

| Skill | Test Date | Score | CEFR Level |
| Reading | 03 December 2018 | 180+ | C1 or above |

Below A1 — A1 — A2 — B1 — B2 — C1 or above

Can understand long and complex texts on a wide range of topics in daily life and work, including unfamiliar and abstract. Can extract key information and details, and comprehend information that is implied. Can detect the writer's tone and point of view.

| Skill | Test Date | Score | CEFR Level |
| Speaking | 05 December 2018 | 148 | B1 |

Below A1 — A1 — A2 — B1 — B2 — C1 or above

Can exchange views on familiar topics, accounting for and sustaining opinions. Can present clear, detailed descriptions on a wide range of topics with a degree of fluency and spontaneity.

4 a CEFR description of what you **can do** for each skill (Reading, Listening, Writing, Speaking)

For more information about test results and an example of a Test Report Form or a Group Report go to

https://www.cambridgeenglish.org/exams-and-tests/linguaskill/information-about-the-test/how-results-are-presented/

What is the format of each test module and what questions or tasks are there?

 Listening and Reading

This is an **adaptive** test so the tasks don't come in a specific order.

Time: There is no fixed time for this module but it may take between 60 and 85 minutes. The test will finish when you have answered enough questions for the computer to identify your English level.

Listening

This part of the test consists of short and longer recordings. You can hear each recording twice.

Example questions/tasks

▷ Listen to different short recordings. For each question, choose one correct option. There are three different options for each question.

▷ Listen to a longer recording. Choose one correct option for each question. The questions are in the same order as the recording.

Reading

This part of the test has short and longer reading texts. You need to understand the texts to answer the questions.

There are also some texts to complete with missing words. This tests you on **language structures** in a text, for example: verbs and tenses, different parts of speech (nouns, adjectives, adverbs, etc), words which connect with others (prepositions), words which connect sentences together, etc.

Example questions/tasks

▷ Read a notice, diagram, label, note, email. Choose the sentence or phrase which gives the best meaning of the text. There is one question with three possible answers.

▷ Read sentences with one missing word. Choose the correct word to complete the gap. There are four different options to choose from for each question.

▷ Read a short text with gaps. Choose the correct word or phrase to complete the gaps. There are four different options to choose from for each question.

▷ Read a short text with gaps. Complete the gaps with one word.

▷ Read a longer text. Choose the correct option to answer the questions. The questions are in the same order as the text.

# Writing

Write your answers into the answer text box on the screen. Your marks are generated automatically and you are guaranteed to get your result within 48 hours. Your overall mark is a combination of your marks for Parts 1 and 2.

Time: 45 minutes

Example questions/tasks

Part 1

Read a short email. Use the information in the text and the three main points to write an email of a minimum of 50 words. Spend about 15 minutes on this part.

Part 2

Read a short text giving you a situation or context and three main points. Use the information and the three points to write an answer of a minimum of 180 words. For Linguaskill General, this piece of writing may be a review or an article. For Linguaskill Business, it could be a report or a letter. Spend about 30 minutes on this part.

Speaking

There are five parts to the Speaking module. You will see some questions on the screen or hear them through headphones. A timer on the screen will show you how long you have to answer questions. In some parts you have time to think and prepare. The computer records your answers and you get your results within 48 hours. Each part is 20% of your final mark.

Time: 15 minutes

Example questions/tasks

Part 1

Answer eight questions about yourself. You will hear the questions. For questions 1–4 you have ten seconds to speak. For questions 5–8 you have 20 seconds to speak. The first two questions aren't marked/graded. In this part you will talk about yourself, your personal experiences, interests, studies or work, future plans, etc.

Part 2

Read eight sentences on the screen. The sentences appear on the screen one by one and you have ten seconds to read each sentence aloud. This part tests pronunciation, including stress, rhythm and intonation.

Part 3

Talk for one minute about a topic. On the screen you can see the topic and three main points to help or guide you. You have 40 seconds to think and prepare before you speak.

Part 4

Talk for one minute about one or more graphics on screen. The graphic may be a chart, a diagram, a process or some information. It stays on the screen when you record your answer. You have one minute to think and prepare. In this part you may need to describe things, compare and contrast things or make recommendations about things.

Part 5

Answer five questions about a topic. You have 40 seconds to read the task explaining the topic and giving you key points on what the questions will be about. You hear the questions and have 20 seconds to answer each question. In this part you need to describe things, give opinions, explain your ideas and give examples to support your ideas.

Linguaskill in the future

Cambridge Assessment English is part of the University of Cambridge and many different institutions and organisations recognise its English language exams around the world. Experts study and update the exams and qualifications regularly because they want to give learners and exam takers the best opportunities to do well with their English.

The three modules of Linguaskill (Listening and Reading, Writing, and Speaking) will become **four** modules in the future and the format will be:

Use of English

This will test grammatical structures and vocabulary. It will be adaptive and the types of questions will be similar to the more grammatical ones in the reading part of the Listening and Reading module, e.g. completing sentences with a word or phrase, or choosing the correct option to complete a text, etc.

Listening and Reading

This will test your understanding of reading and recorded texts with comprehension questions, e.g. choose the correct answer from a choice of three options.

Writing

There will be one question. The style of writing will be similar to the existing Writing module, e.g. emails, reports, letters.

Speaking

The format and different parts will be similar to the existing Speaking module.

Preparing for and taking Linguaskill

Key points to remember: General

▶ Make sure you know about the test format.

- How many modules are you taking?
- What do they test?
- How many parts are there in a specific module, e.g. Speaking or Writing?
- What types of questions are there?
- How much time do you have for each module, e.g. Speaking or Writing?
- Do you have any time to think and prepare?
- Check you know about **the timing** for each module or part of a test, e.g. Speaking and Writing.
- There is a clock on the computer screen which shows you how much time you have for some modules.
- If the test module doesn't have a fixed time (e.g. the Listening and Reading module), check if the place where you take the test will set a time on the computer screen. Find out before you take the test!

▶ Read all the instructions for each part of the test carefully. They are there to help you.

▶ Use any online resources to practise taking the test modules before you take the real test. This will help you to become familiar with the test and questions in each part. (See **Useful links for the Linguaskill test** on page 2 for more information.)

▶ Try to answer all the questions and make a guess, even if you aren't sure.

▶ Try to write and speak as much as you can in the time you have in the Writing and Speaking modules.

Preparing for and taking Linguaskill

Key points to remember: Specific Linguaskill modules

 ### Listening and Reading

▶ Remember, the computer will give you easier or harder questions based on how you have answered a previous question.

▶ You cannot go back or forward to look at questions or to check your answers because the test is online and adaptive.

▶ Don't worry if some questions seem difficult or you think you haven't answered a question correctly. Always try to answer and the computer will **adapt** the questions to your level of English.

▶ In the Listening module, speakers often talk about **all** the things in the pictures or task options but not necessarily in the same order. Only **one** picture or option is correct based on what the speakers say.

▶ There is a longer reading text and listening section in this module with multiple choice questions. Don't worry if you can't answer all the questions the first time. Remember that with the listening, you can hear each recording twice.

▶ Don't worry if another person taking the test finishes and leaves the room before you. Remember, this module **doesn't have a fixed time**.

✐ Writing

▶ Read all the instructions and the information to answer the question first.

▶ Make sure you know what type of text you need to write, e.g. an email, a report, etc.

▶ You can make notes in the answer text box to answer the question but remember to delete any notes you make on screen before you submit your answer.

▶ You can cut and paste parts of your answer using the cut and paste buttons above the answer text box. You can also use Ctrl + C/X/V to do this.

▶ Don't spend time counting the words you write. There is a word count at the bottom of the computer writing screen that does this for you.

▶ Use the information for the task and the three main points to help you structure your writing.

▶ Try to write as much as you can to show what you can do.

▶ Spend about 3–5 minutes checking your piece of writing before you submit it. Check: the style of writing, spelling, punctuation, grammatical structures, words and phrases.

🎧 Speaking

▶ Before you start the test check your headphones and the microphone. Try to speak clearly and keep the microphone the same distance from your mouth throughout the test.

▶ Use all of the time you have for each part of the test and say as much as you can.

▶ You will hear a sound to tell you when to start and stop speaking. Don't worry if the computer stops you in the middle of your answer.

Example questions, tasks and tips

In this section there are different types of questions or tasks that may appear in the Linguaskill General and Business test. Remember, they are *examples*. The tips are to guide you and help you think about how to answer the questions.

For examples of test practice materials that you can use to practise taking the test go to
https://www.cambridgeenglish.org/exams-and-tests/linguaskill/information-about-the-test/practice-materials/

Listening and Reading

Listening example: Question 1

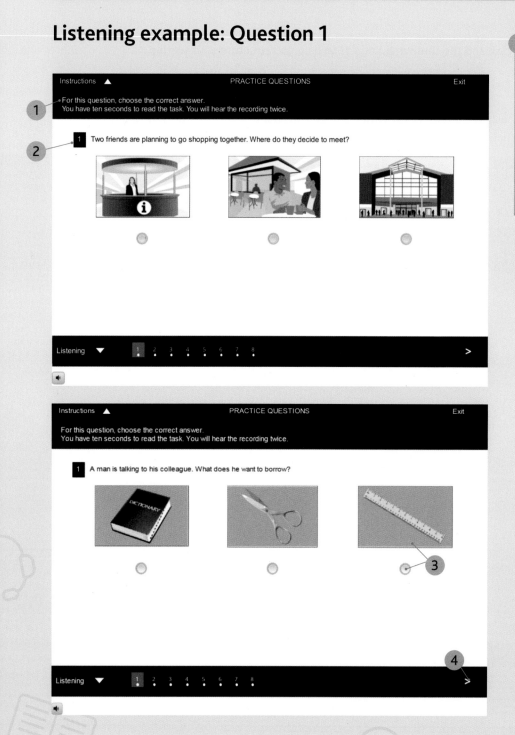

1 Always read the instructions carefully. You have time to look at the pictures or read the questions first.

- How many times can you hear the recording?
- How many question options are there?

2 Read the question carefully.

- Who is talking?
- What are they talking about?
- What can you see in the pictures?

3 Listen carefully. The second time you listen, choose only one answer and click on the button.

4 If you're sure about your answer the first time, don't listen again. Click on the arrow and go to the next question.

Listening and Reading

Listening example: Question 2

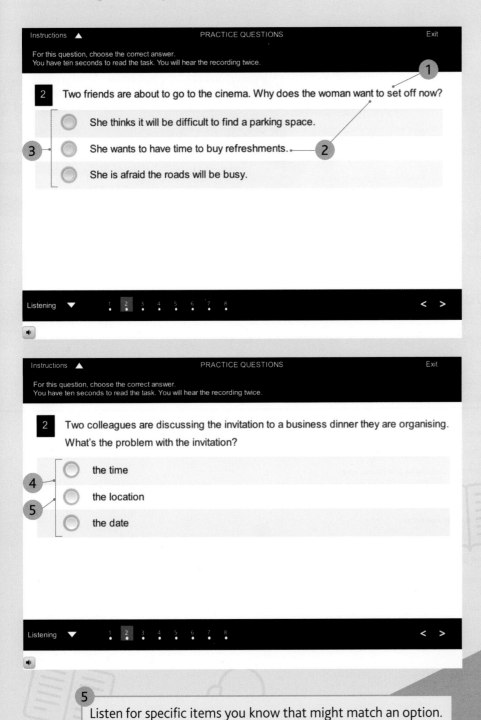

1 Look for key words in the question, e.g. *Two friends are about to go to the cinema*. Now find key words in the second example question.

2 Read the complete question and options. Try and guess any words you might not know.
Why does the woman want to set off now?
She wants to have time to buy refreshments.
Does *set off* mean a) not go or b) leave now?
Does *refreshments* mean a) something to eat or drink b) the best seats?

3 Listen for words you know in the conversation first. Try to match them to the question options.
Match these words to a question option: *drink, popcorn, big car park, traffic, heavier*

4 Remember, there is only one possible answer. Click on one option before you go to the next question.

5 Listen for specific items you know that might match an option. Match these items to an option: *at 8, at the Carlton, the 15ᵗʰ, at 7, the 14ᵗʰ*

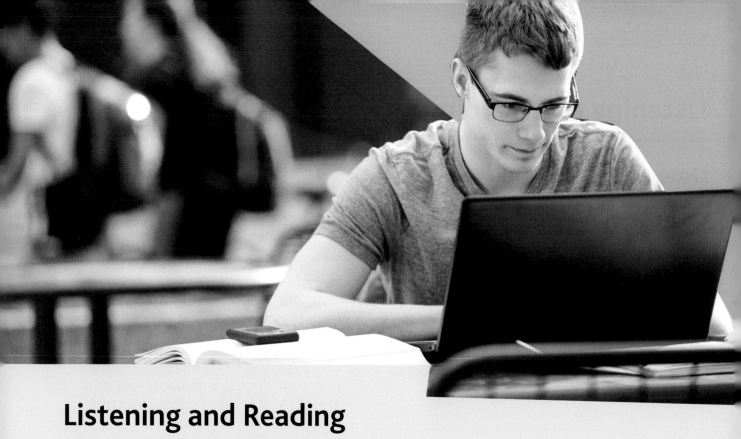

Listening and Reading

Listening example: Question 3

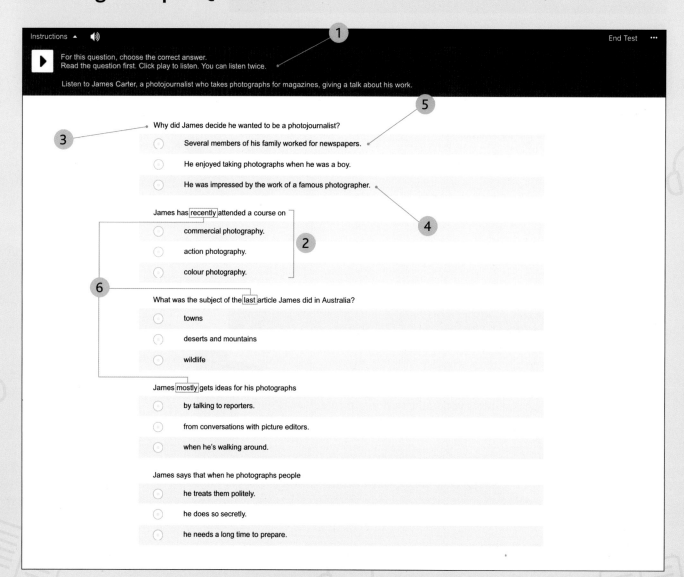

Instructions ▲ 🔊   ①   End Test ⋯

▶ For this question, choose the correct answer.
Read the question first. Click play to listen. You can listen twice.

Listen to James Carter, a photojournalist who takes photographs for magazines, giving a talk about his work.

⑤

Why did James decide he wanted to be a photojournalist?

③

  ◯   Several members of his family worked for newspapers.

  ◯   He enjoyed taking photographs when he was a boy.

  ◯   He was impressed by the work of a famous photographer.

④

James has recently attended a course on

  ◯   commercial photography.

②

  ◯   action photography.

  ◯   colour photography.

⑥

What was the subject of the last article James did in Australia?

  ◯   towns

  ◯   deserts and mountains

  ◯   wildlife

James mostly gets ideas for his photographs

  ◯   by talking to reporters.

  ◯   from conversations with picture editors.

  ◯   when he's walking around.

James says that when he photographs people

  ◯   he treats them politely.

  ◯   he does so secretly.

  ◯   he needs a long time to prepare.

1 You have time to read the questions before you listen. You can start the recording when <u>you</u> are ready.

2 The speakers will talk about all the things in the options but not always in the same order.

3 Read the main part of the question first. Find key words to help you focus on each question.

<u>Why</u> did James decide he <u>wanted</u> to be a <u>photojournalist</u>?

Now find key words in the main part of other questions.

4 Read the question options carefully. Find more key words in the options, e.g.

He was <u>impressed</u> by the <u>work</u> of a <u>famous photographer</u>.

5 Listen for words or phrases which are similar to words in the questions, e.g. *grandfather, father, mother = Q1: several members of his family.*

Try and match these words or phrases from the recording to parts of the questions:

advertising,

the pictures were so exciting,

…without them knowing,

the last feature,

set up well

6 Check and listen for any words, phrases or language structures which may help you choose an answer.

Match these words to two of the words in the questions:

the majority,

just

Match these phrases to different question options:

As a boy, I wanted to do something different.

If you take too long, people won't be relaxed.

Before, I'd been concentrating on wildlife.

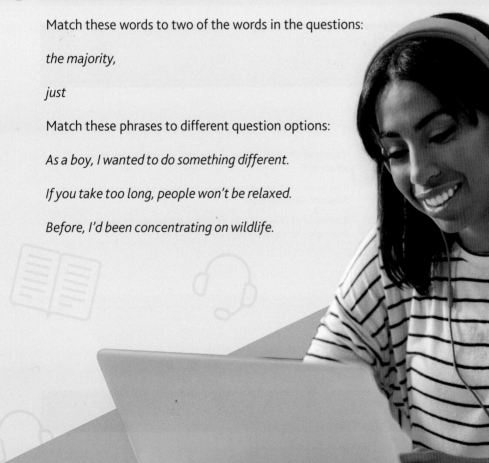

Listening and Reading

Reading example: Question 1

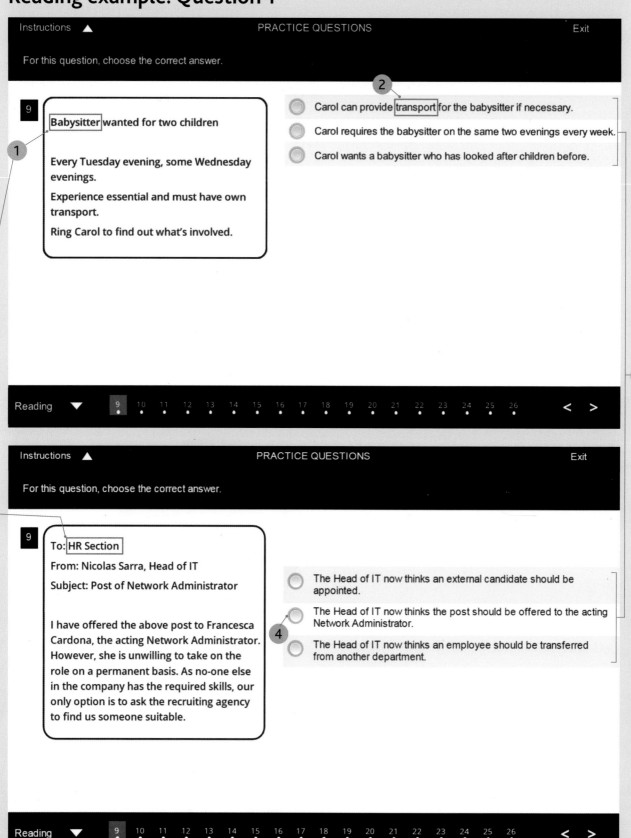

Instructions ▲   PRACTICE QUESTIONS   Exit

For this question, choose the correct answer.

9

Babysitter wanted for two children

Every Tuesday evening, some Wednesday evenings.

Experience essential and must have own transport.

Ring Carol to find out what's involved.

- ○ Carol can provide transport for the babysitter if necessary.
- ○ Carol requires the babysitter on the same two evenings every week.
- ○ Carol wants a babysitter who has looked after children before.

Reading ▼   **9** 10 11 12 13 14 15 16 17 18 19 20 21 22 23 24 25 26   < >

Instructions ▲   PRACTICE QUESTIONS   Exit

For this question, choose the correct answer.

9

To: HR Section

From: Nicolas Sarra, Head of IT

Subject: Post of Network Administrator

I have offered the above post to Francesca Cardona, the acting Network Administrator. However, she is unwilling to take on the role on a permanent basis. As no-one else in the company has the required skills, our only option is to ask the recruiting agency to find us someone suitable.

- ○ The Head of IT now thinks an external candidate should be appointed.
- ○ The Head of IT now thinks the post should be offered to the acting Network Administrator.
- ○ The Head of IT now thinks an employee should be transferred from another department.

Reading ▼   **9** 10 11 12 13 14 15 16 17 18 19 20 21 22 23 24 25 26   < >

1   Read the notice or message quickly first.

- What is it about?

- Who is it for?

2   Read the three options in the questions quickly. Find any words in the options that are in the text, e.g. *transport*.

Find more words in the text and options.

3   Look for words or phrases in the options that connect to parts of the text. Find similar or different meanings.

GE option 1: <u>can provide</u> transport > *<u>must have own</u> transport*. Different.

Are these examples similar or different?

- GE option 2: the <u>same</u> two evenings <u>every</u> week > *<u>Every</u> Tuesday evening, <u>some</u> Wednesday evenings*

- GE option 3: <u>has looked after</u> children <u>before</u> > *experience essential*

- BE option 1: an <u>external</u> candidate <u>should be appointed</u> > *ask recruiting agency to <u>find</u> someone*

- BE option 3: an <u>employee</u> <u>should be transferred</u> > *no-one else in the company has the required skills*

4   Try to guess the meaning of words you might not know.

BE option 2: the post <u>should be offered</u> to the acting Network administrator

However, she is <u>unwilling</u> to take on the role.

Does *unwilling* mean a) interested b) not interested?

What word in the sentence means *but*?

Listening and Reading

Reading example: Question 2

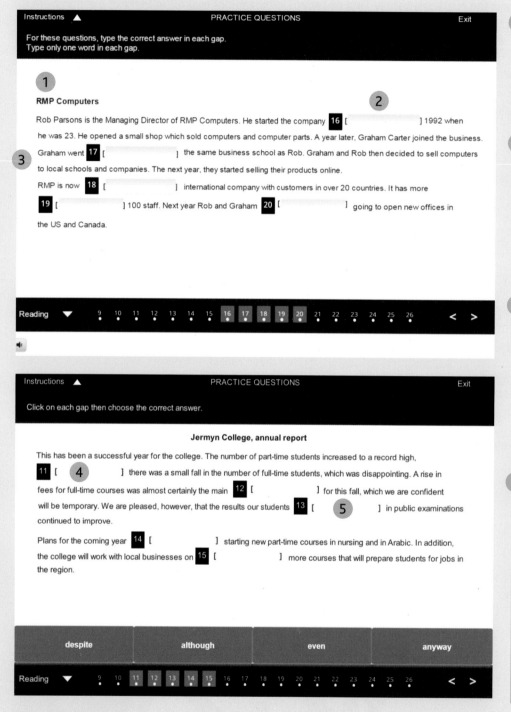

1
Read the whole text quickly first and don't worry about the gaps. What is it about?

2
Remember, there is **only one answer** for each gap in the text.
Write **one word** to complete the gap where a word is missing.

3
Decide what part of speech is missing from each gap. Do this before you look at any options, e.g. a noun, verb, adjective, adverb, preposition, etc.

4
Try putting each option in the gap. Eliminate any you think are definitely wrong.
Look at Jermyn College Q11: Which options are <u>not</u> possible? Think about grammar:
despite there was
although there was
even there was
anyway there was

5
Check any words **before** and **after** the gaps. They may help you choose your answer.
Look at Jermyn College Q13: Which nouns go with the verbs *achieve, win, complete, reach*?
a prize / a project / a conclusion / results

Listening and Reading

Reading example: Question 3

1 Scroll down and read the whole text quickly to get a general idea first.

2 Look at the main part of each question first. If they are questions, try to answer them before you look at the options.

3 Eliminate any options that are wrong, e.g. Q21 option 3: It <u>has had sales</u> of 50 million this year. The text says it <u>*is on target to hit sales* of 50 million this year.</u>

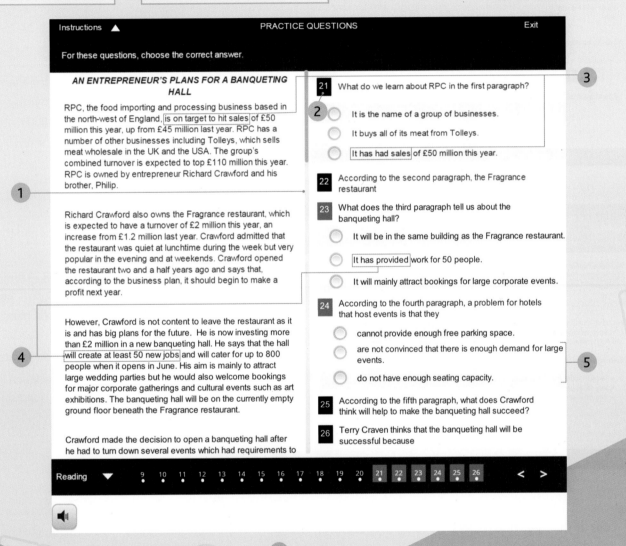

4 Pay attention to verb tenses in the options and the text. Do a true or false test on the options, e.g. Q23 option 2: It <u>has provided</u> work for 50 people. The text says it <u>*will create* at least 50 new jobs year.</u>

5 Pay attention to questions that may have opinions or facts.

Look at Q24 options 2 and 3:

- **Who** thinks there isn't a demand for big events at hotels?
- What does **Crawford** think?
- What does he say about the number of seats most hotels have for big events?
- Is option 2 or 3 correct?

Writing

Writing example tasks: Part 1

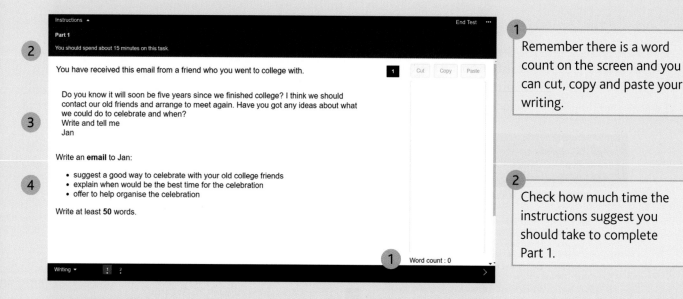

2 **3** **4**

1 Remember there is a word count on the screen and you can cut, copy and paste your writing.

2 Check how much time the instructions suggest you should take to complete Part 1.

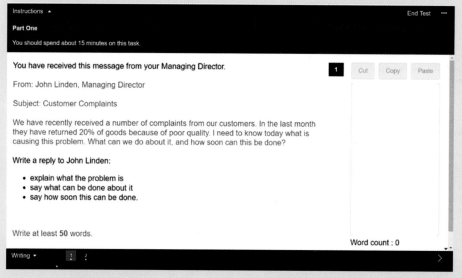

3 Read the instructions and the text. Check:

Who you are writing to and why

What type of text you need to write

How much you need to write

Now check this information in the second example question.

4 Look at the three main points. Try to think of useful phrases to include when you write.

- **Suggest** *Why don't we…? What about…+ -ing? We could…*

- **Explain** *I think it would be best to / The best time would be… because…*

- **Offer** *I can/could help… If you want me to… I'll… Would you like me to…?*

Now do the same for the second example question.

5 Before you submit your answer, check spelling, punctuation, grammatical structures, words and expressions, and the style.

Writing

Writing example tasks: Part 2

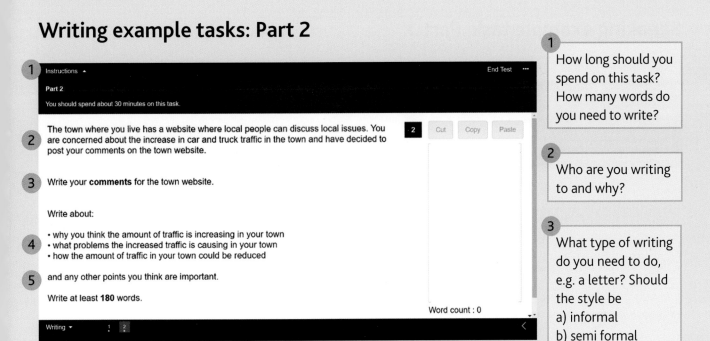

1 How long should you spend on this task? How many words do you need to write?

2 Who are you writing to and why?

3 What type of writing do you need to do, e.g. a letter? Should the style be
a) informal
b) semi formal
c) formal?

4 What useful phrases can you use to structure ideas for the three points?

For example, question 1 – why you think the amount of traffic is increasing in your town:

I think…, I believe…, In my opinion…

Try to add some more phrases for each point in both examples.

5 You need to try and include more ideas of your own. What information could you add to answer the question?

For example, bullet point 3 – how the amount of traffic in your town could be reduced:

make public transport cheaper and more frequent, close off specific areas to cars and trucks, create more cycle and walking lanes

Try to add some more ideas for both examples.

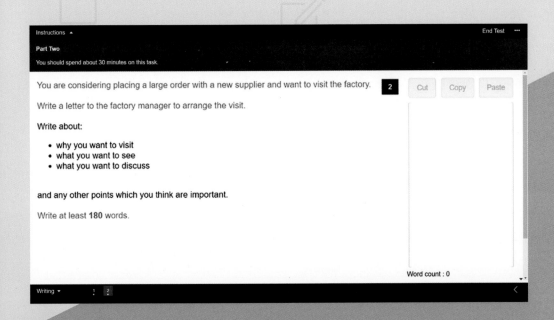

Speaking

Speaking example task: Part 1

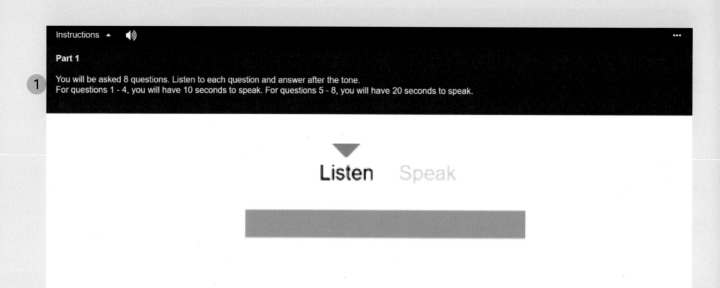

Instructions ▲ 🔊 ⋯

Part 1

You will be asked 8 questions. Listen to each question and answer after the tone.
For questions 1 - 4, you will have 10 seconds to speak. For questions 5 - 8, you will have 20 seconds to speak.

▼

Listen Speak

Part 1 General English

1 What's your name?

2 How do you spell your family name?

3 Where are you from?

4 Do you work or are you a student?

5 What do you enjoy doing at weekends?

6 Do you get many opportunities to speak English?

7 What's the best thing that happened to you last week?

8 Where would you like to live in the future?

Part 1 Business English

1 What's your name?

2 How do you spell your family name?

3 Where are you from?

4 What's your job?

5 How long have you been with your present company?

6 How do you use English in your work?

7 What are the opportunities for promotion in your current job?

8 What will you do at work next week?

1. Read and listen to the instructions carefully for **all parts of the test**.

   - How many questions are there?

   - How much time do you have to answer a) questions 1–4   b) questions 5–8?

2. Remember the first two questions aren't assessed. They are to help you *warm up* for the test.

3. Remember, you will **hear** the questions; they won't be on the screen.

4. Look at the two sets of questions. Find different verb tenses you can use in your answers.

   For example,

   GE Q7: past simple tense for finished activities

   BE Q5: present perfect simple tense for activities which started in the past but continue now

5. Remember to try and say as much as you can in **all parts of the test** in the time you have.

6. Practise answering the different questions in the time you have. Time yourself.

Speaking

Speaking example task: Part 2

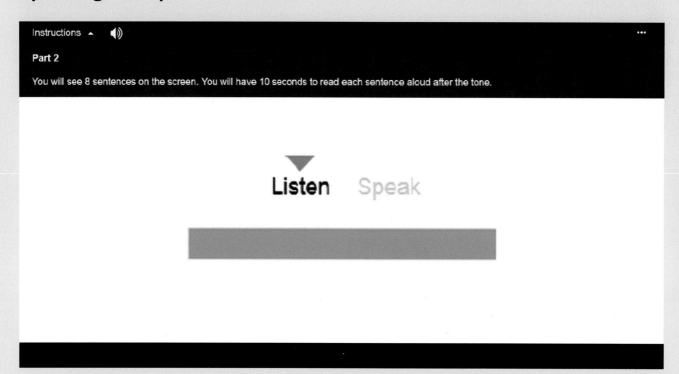

> **Part 2 General English (Sentences on screen)**
>
> 1 The library is closed for staff training until 11am.
>
> 2 Mrs Hill would like to accept the invitation.
>
> 3 The bus timetable can sometimes change at short notice.
>
> 4 Thank you for coming to the film club's summer event.
>
> 5 How easy will it be for students to find accommodation near the university?
>
> 6 After you have finished making online payments, remember to log out of your account.
>
> 7 A 'UV index' reading of 11 indicates an extreme risk of harm from the sun's rays.
>
> 8 On average there are twice as many applicants for undergraduate degree courses as places available.

Part 2 Business English (Sentences on screen)

1   The team needs sales staff who can speak more than one language.

2   The 5% discount is only on orders over $10,000.

3   Have the long-term goals of the company changed?

4   Your account will become active on receipt of the first payment.

5   Mrs Atkins called to say that she is away at a marketing conference this week.

6   The R&D budget has been frozen for five years but will increase again next January.

7   The organisation, which has its headquarters in Canada, has now expanded into many European countries.

8   The best way to reduce distribution costs is to use our subsidiary to transport goods.

---

1 This part of the test focuses on pronunciation, including stress, rhythm and intonation.

2 Practise saying numbers, money and the letters of the alphabet before the test.

Say the numbers, times, signs (%, $) and individual letters in GE Q1 and Q7 and BE Q2 and Q6.

3 Before the test check and practise sounds or stress in individual words you find in sentences.

For example, GE Q2 invi**ta**tion, BE Q2 **dis**count, GE Q4 cl**u**b (*u*), BE Q1 langu**age** (ɪdʒ)

Say these words: *notice, accommodation, extreme, average, conference, increase* (verb), *January, headquarters, Canada, distribution*

4 Some sentences may look difficult or long. Look for punctuation (e.g. commas) which helps you pause when you speak. Try to pace yourself and speak as clearly as you can.

- Practise reading GE Q6 and BE Q7. Use the commas to help you pause naturally when you speak.

- Practise reading GE Q8 and BE Q8.

- Try to find places in the sentence where you can pause and then continue, e.g.
On average / there are twice as many applicants / for undergraduate degree courses / as places available.

5 Practise saying the sentences in the time you have. Time yourself.

Speaking

Speaking example tasks: Part 3

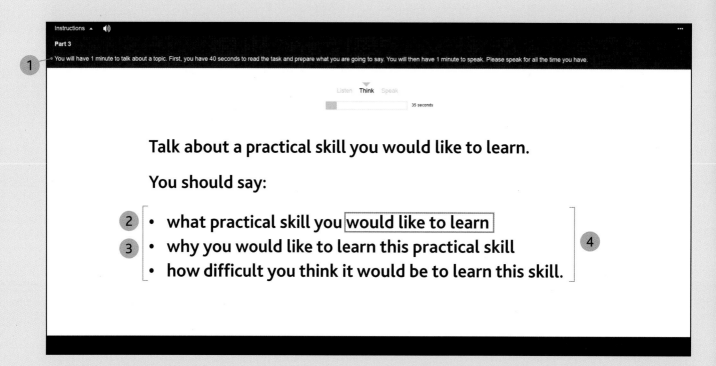

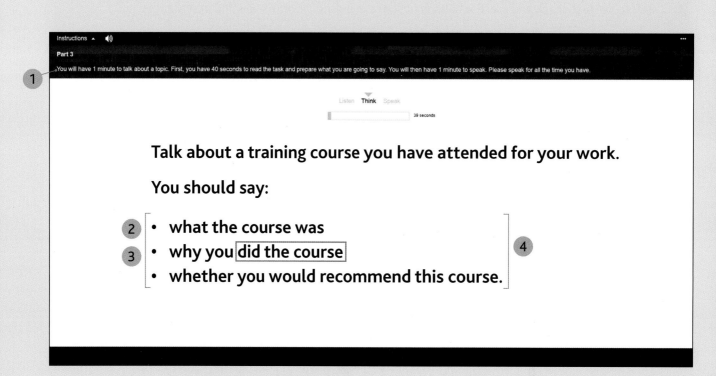

1. Read the instructions carefully. How much time do you have to

   a) prepare   b) answer?

2. Read the topic and the three main points carefully. Check any verb tenses in the main points.

   - What tenses or structures can you see in the main points for the question?

   - What wh- question words are there, e.g. *what, how*, etc?

3. Check if you need to explain or describe, give a reason, give your opinion, recommend, etc.

   For example, BE point 1: *explain about / describe the course*

   Find other examples in the main points.

4. Find any words or phrases from the main points to structure your ideas. Think of other phrases you can use.

   For example, GE main points:

   I'd like to learn…because…

   I think it would be a useful skill to learn because…

   It might be difficult but…

   Think of more phrases for both tasks.

5. You can make some notes on paper if you want

6. Practise talking about one or both of the topics for one minute. Time yourself.

Speaking

Speaking example tasks: Part 4

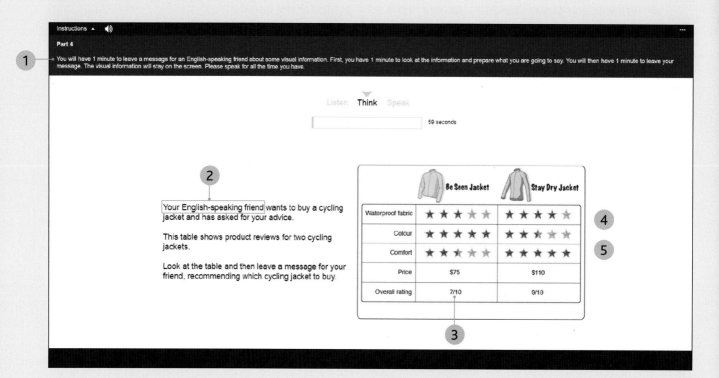

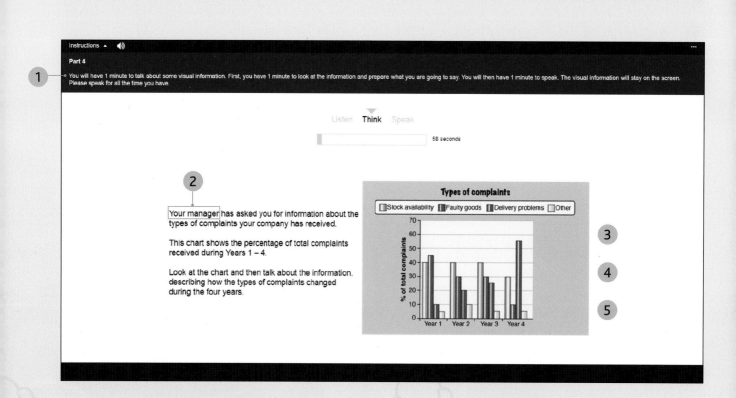

1   Read the instructions carefully. How much time do you have to

      a) prepare   b) answer?

2   Read the information carefully.

      a) Who are you speaking to?   b) What about?

      Look at the information you can see in the graph or chart. Remember it will stay on screen when you record your answer.

3   Check for any numbers, facts or symbols, e.g. *seven out of 10, more than / less than 10 percent*

      Practise saying the numbers, facts and symbols in the graphs.

4   Check for any words or phrases you might not know. Can you guess their meaning? How do you say them?

5   Think about any useful language structures:

      •   to compare or contrast the information, e.g. *both, whereas, while*

      •   to recommend things or give an opinion, e.g. *I'd recommend… because, I think / don't think… because*

      •   words / expressions to connect your ideas, e.g. *but, and, so, however*

      Can you add any more ideas?

6   Practise talking about one or both of the topics for one minute. Time yourself.

Speaking

Speaking example tasks: Part 5

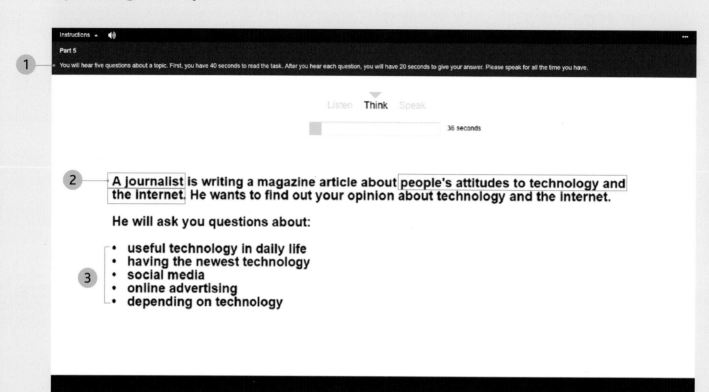

Instructions ▲ 🔊

Part 5

You will hear five questions about a topic. First, you have 40 seconds to read the task. After you hear each question, you will have 20 seconds to give your answer. Please speak for all the time you have.

Listen   **Think**   Speak

36 seconds

A journalist is writing a magazine article about **people's attitudes to technology and the internet.** He wants to find out your opinion about technology and the internet.

He will ask you questions about:

- **useful technology in daily life**
- **having the newest technology**
- **social media**
- **online advertising**
- **depending on technology**

Part 5 General English (possible questions)

1 Which technology do you think is most useful to people in their daily life?

2 How important do you think it is to have the newest technology?

3 In your opinion, is social media a good thing or a bad thing?

4 How do you think people feel about online advertising?

5 Some people say we depend too much on technology. What do you think?

1
Read the instructions carefully. How much time do you have to a) prepare b) answer?

2
Read the information carefully.
a) Who are you speaking to?
b) What about?

3
There are five main points for each task.

Try to think of a question for each point in about 40 seconds. Use *Wh-* question words and any key words in the points to help you. Time yourself. Then compare your ideas with the test questions. For example, GE point 1 *What technology is useful in daily life?* BE point 1 *What benefits are there for companies that offer sponsorship?*

Instructions ▲ 🔊

Part 5

You will hear five questions about a topic. First, you have 40 seconds to read the task. After you hear each question, you will have 20 seconds to give your answer. Please speak for all the time you have.

Listen **Think** Speak

40 seconds

2

A business owner is thinking about using sponsorship to publicise his company. He wants to find out your opinion about **the best way to organise a sponsorship programme.**

He will ask you questions about:

3
- **benefits for companies**
- **who to sponsor**
- **length of sponsorship**
- **possible problems**
- **judging success**

4

Part 5 Business English (possible questions)

1   In your opinion, what are the benefits of companies offering sponsorship?

2   Would it be better to sponsor an individual or an organisation?

3   How long should a sponsorship programme last?

4   What problems could there be with a sponsorship programme?

5   How could a company judge whether its sponsorship has been successful?

4
The questions often ask you about your opinion. Think of words or useful phrases for giving your opinion, giving reasons why and adding any information, e.g. *I think/don't think that… I'm (quite/fairly/not) sure that… because… This means that… This is why…*

Can you add any more ideas?

5
Some questions may ask you to speculate. Think of any useful words or phrases, e.g. *could, might, may (not)*, etc.

Can you add any more ideas?

6
Practise answering the questions about one or both of the topics for one minute. Time yourself.

Example tasks and tips answer key

Listening

Example Question 1

1
twice
2
three
3
1 Two friends / Where to meet to go shopping together. / An information desk, people in a café, a conference centre
2 A man and his colleague. / Something he wants to borrow. / A dictionary, scissors, a ruler

Example Question 2

1 Suggested answer
<u>Two colleagues</u> are <u>discussing</u> the <u>invitation</u> to a <u>business dinner</u> they are <u>organising</u>. What's the <u>problem</u> with the <u>invitation?</u>
2
b/a
3
Option 1: *big car park* Option 2: *drink, popcorn* Option 3: *traffic, heavier*
5
Option 1: *at 8, at 7* Option 2: *at the Carlton* Option 3: *the 15th, the 14th*

Example Question 3

3
Suggested answers
1 James has <u>recently</u> <u>attended a course</u> on
2 What was <u>the subject</u> of the <u>last article</u> James did <u>in Australia?</u>
3 James <u>mostly</u> <u>gets ideas</u> for his <u>photographs</u>
4 James says that <u>when</u> he <u>photographs people</u>
4
Suggested answers
1
<u>Several members</u> of his <u>family</u> <u>worked</u> for <u>newspapers</u>
He <u>enjoyed</u> <u>taking photographs</u> <u>when</u> he <u>was a boy</u>
2
<u>commercial</u> photography
<u>action</u> photography
<u>colour</u> photography
3
<u>towns</u>
<u>deserts</u> and <u>mountains</u>
<u>wildlife</u>

4
by <u>talking</u> to <u>reporters</u>
from conversations with <u>picture editors</u>
when he's <u>walking around</u>
5
he <u>treats them politely</u>
he <u>does so secretly</u>
he <u>needs</u> a <u>long time</u> to <u>prepare</u>
5
Question 2 option 1: *advertising,*
Question 1 option 3: *the pictures were so exciting, …*
Question 5 option 2: *without them knowing,*
Question 3 main question part: *the last feature,*
Question 5 option 3: *set up well*
6
The majority = mostly
Just = recently
Question 1 option 2: *As a boy, I wanted to do something different*
Question 5 option 3: *If you take too long, people won't be relaxed*
Question 3 option 3: *Before, I'd been concentrating on wildlife*

Reading

Example Question 1

1
1 Babysitting / someone who wants to babysit.
2 The post for a network administrator / someone in the Human Resources section.
2 *babysitter, every, evening(s), children*
3
GE option 2: the <u>same</u> two evenings <u>every</u> week > *Every Tuesday evening, some Wednesday evenings.* **Different**
GE option 3: <u>has looked after</u> children <u>before</u> > *experience essential* **Similar**
BE option 1: an <u>external</u> candidate <u>should be appointed</u> > *ask recruiting agency to find someone* **Similar**
BE option 3: an <u>employee</u> <u>should be transferred</u> > *no-one else in the company has the required skills* **Different**
4
Unwilling means b)
However means *but*

Example Question 2

1
1 The story of a computer company
2 A college annual report

4
1
despite there was **X** despite + *-ing*
although there was **correct**
even there was **X** *even* **though** *there was*
anyway there was **X** would need punctuation and is more spoken, informal style *Anyway, there was…*
5
achieve results, win a prize, complete a project, reach a conclusion

Example Question 3

5
1 Some people / Crawford thinks they are wrong.
2 Most hotels don't have seats for more than about 500 people. Option 3 is correct.

Writing

Example tasks Part 1

3
1 Your managing director about customer complaints.
2 An email message.
3 At least 50 words.
5
Suggested answers
1 *One thing that can/could be done is… Another way to improve is… We can remedy the situation by…*
2 *The problem is…, What seems to have happened is… I think the reason for this is…*
3 *We'll make sure that this is done as soon as possible, We'll carry out these action points immediately*

Example tasks Part 2

1
1 about 30 minutes, at least 180 words
2
1 GE: a town website / to discuss the increase in car and truck traffic in town
2 BE: to the factory manager / to arrange a visit
3
1 GE: comments to the town website / semi formal
2 BE: a letter / semi formal to formal
4
Suggested answers
1 GE:
1 *From what I understand…, As far as I know… It seems to be/could be… The increase in traffic is due to… It's because…*

It's the result of… One of reasons why it's increasing is…
2 *This is causing…and also…, As a result, some of the problems are… We can see that…and consequently…*
3 *I'd like to suggest that… One of the ways we could…is/might be… I really believe that…if the council*
2 BE:
1 *I would like/I'd like to arrange a visit because/in order to…, It would be useful to visit…so that…*
2 *I would like/I'd like to visit/see…if possible/if it's not inconvenient because… Would it be possible to have access to… because…*
3 *I would/I'd like to talk about/discuss the issue of/some points about… Would you mind putting…on the agenda for discussion?*
5
Suggested answers
1 GE: *walk and cycle more, restrict times for trucks to travel through the town, recommend the town council creates an online information site to encourage people to use public transport…*
2 BE: *build in time during the visit to discuss the delivery dates, any special discounts, etc.*

Speaking

Example task Part 1

1
1 eight
2 a) 10 seconds b) 20 seconds
4
1 GE: Q1–Q6: present simple for facts and routines, Q8: *would like* for preferences
2 BE: Q1–Q4, Q6, Q7: present simple for facts and routines, Q8 *will* for future facts

Example task Part 2

3
no*tice*, accommo*dation*, ex*treme*, *average*, *conference*, *increase (verb)*, **J**anuary, head*quarters*, **C**anada, distri*bution*

Example tasks Part 3

1
a) forty seconds b) one minute
2
1 GE: *would like* for preferences and *would* for hypothesis/what, why, how
2 BE: past simple for completed actions and *would like* for preferences/what, why, whether
3
1 GE: describe, give preferences, give reasons why, give your opinion
2 BE: describe, explain, give reasons why, make recommendations

4
1 GE: *I've never tried…so…, It's a really important skill because…, I don't think it would be too difficult because…*
2 BE: *The course was about…, I chose to do this course because…, I'd definitely recommend it because… I wouldn't suggest doing this type of course because…*

Example tasks Part 4

1
a) one minute b) one minute
2
1 GE: a) an English speaking friend
b) a cycling jacket
2 BE: a) your manager b) complaints your company has received
4
1 GE:
waterproof: not allowing water to go through
rating: how good or popular someone or something is
2 BE:
stock availability: a supply of something that you can buy or get
faulty: does not work correctly
5
1 *one similarity/difference is… X is (a bit/a lot/much/more… than… Y isn't as… as.*
2 *X seems, might be/have, Y is probably better than, I'm (not) sure that…*
3 *also, on the one/other hand*

Example tasks Part 5

1
a) forty seconds b) 20 seconds
2
1 GE: a) a journalist b) people's attitudes to the internet
2 BE: a) a business owner b) the best way to organise a sponsorship programme
3
Suggested answers
GE
2 Why do people want to have the newest technology?
3 What are the advantages and disadvantages of social media?
4 What do you think about online advertising?
5 Do you think we depend too much on technology?
BE
2 Who is it better to sponsor, a company or an individual?
3 How long should you sponsor a company or an individual?
4 What possible problems are there with sponsorship?
5 How can you decide if sponsorship has been a success?

4
Suggested answers
I guess/reckon that… so, I'd say that… apart from this… I'd like to add that…
5
Suggested answers
seems (to be/have), I imagine that… It's unlikely that… The chances are that…

Acknowledgements

The authors and publishers acknowledge the following sources of copyright material and are grateful for the permissions granted. While every effort has been made, it has not always been possible to identify the sources of all the material used, or to trace all copyright holders. If any omissions are brought to our notice, we will be happy to include the appropriate acknowledgements on reprinting and in the next update to the digital edition, as applicable.

Photographs

The following photographs are sourced from Getty Images.

Overview of the Linguaskill test: Navee Sangvitoon/EyeEm; insta_photos/iStock/Getty Images Plus; katleho Seisa/E+; Peopleimages/E+; **Linguaskill in the future**: Peopleimages/E+; **Preparing for and taking Linguaskill:** SamuelBrownNG/iStock/Getty Images Plus; Hill Street Studios/DigitalVision; **Example questions, tasks and tips (Listening and Reading):** AJ_Watt/E+; yacobchuk/iStock/Getty Images Plus; recep-bg/E+; **Example questions, tasks and tips (Speaking):** SDI Productions/E+; PeopleImages/E+; damircudic/V44iStock/Getty Images Plus.

The following photographs are sourced from other sources.

Overview of the Linguaskill test: Screenshot from Linguaskill test report. Copyright © Cambridge Assessment; **Example questions, tasks and tips (Listening and Reading):** Screenshot from Linguaskill listening question 1, page 1. Copyright © Cambridge Assessment; Screenshot from Linguaskill Business practice tests. Copyright © Cambridge Assessment; Screenshot from Linguaskill free online sample test. Copyright © Cambridge Assessment; Screenshot from Linguaskill General practice tests. Copyright © Cambridge Assessment; **Example questions, tasks and tips (Writing):** Screenshot from Linguaskill online practice material General English writing. Copyright © Cambridge Assessment; Screenshot from Linguaskill online practice material Business English writing. Copyright © Cambridge Assessment; **Example questions, tasks and tips (Speaking):** Screenshots of part 1, 2, 3, 4 & 5 from Linguaskill general speaking test. Copyright © Cambridge Assessment; Screenshots of part 3, 4 & 5 from Linguaskill Business speaking test. Copyright © Cambridge Assessment.

Cover photography is designed and illustrated by Crush Creative.

Design and Typeset

IOC Design team